The World of Nature

BACKYARD BIRDS

GALLERY BOOKS

An Imprint of W. H. Smith Publishers Inc.

112 Madison Avenue

New York City 10016

j 598
SCH.

This edition first published in U.S.
in 1990 by Gallery Books,
an imprint of W.H. Smith Publishers, Inc.
112 Madison Avenue, New York, New York 10016

ISBN 0-8317-9582-4

Printed and bound in Spain

For rights information about the photographs in
this book please contact:

The Image Bank
111 Fifth Avenue, New York, NY 10003

Producer: Solomon M. Skolnick
Author: Marcus Schneck
Design Concept: Leslie Ehlers
Designer: Ann-Louise Lipman
Editor: Madelyn Larsen
Production: Valerie Zars
Photo Researcher: Edward Douglas
Assistant Photo Researcher: Robert Hale

Title page: The eastern bluebird is
popular among birders; it has a distinc-
tive, musical call. *Opposite:* The screech
owl can be found anywhere in the United
States. *Overleaf:* A great horned owl
watches over its ungainly chick.

The great horned owl is among the earliest nesting birds in North America, generally laying its eggs in late January or early February. *Below:* Prey in sight, it prepares to swoop in for the kill. The owl preys on everything from insects to lizards to rabbits and grouse.

A saw-whet owl settles onto a nighttime perch, where it will await its prey. *Right:* Barn owls frequent man's structures, hence their name. They rely on an acute sense of hearing in their nightly hunts.

The whiskered owl, a resident primarily of mountain canyons, feeds primarily on insects and scorpions. *Below:* The common nighthawk, also known as the nightjar, takes its prey—flying insects—on the wing. A single bird will consume several hundred insects in a day. *Opposite:* Normally a bird of the North, the hawk-owl sometimes moves south in the winter and can be seen at the edges of fields, vigilantly watching for small birds and rodents.

At the very back of my small backyard, nestled into the row of hemlock trees, is a very special bird feeder. It belongs to a pair of northern cardinals that I know so well. I put it there and keep it filled with seed. It exists for only one reason, to service those two cardinals.

Few creatures can brighten the dismal days of midwinter like these birds. The male's bright red plumage and orange-yellow bill always seem to hold out hope for the more colorful world that is just around the corner, waiting the warming gestation of spring.

The pair of birds are permanent residents of the backyard, and the adjacent backyards of a few neighbors. I've watched them for all of the few years I've lived in this house. Last summer I was privileged to experience their ceaseless efforts to fledge one of the three chicks that they had hatched.

But until I put up that special feeder and filled it with a 50-50 mix of safflower and oil-sunflower seeds, the cardinals were only occasional visitors to my property.

Through the generations they have learned that the same bright feathers that make them so appealing also can serve as a bull's-eye for predators, such as hawks and cats. They visit the other feeders in the backyard at times, but in these exposed locations they spend only brief, nervous moments to grab a seed or two and flit back to the safe cover of the evergreens.

Barn swallows nest in colonies ranging from only a couple pair to several thousand, with most of the females laying their eggs at nearly the same time. *Below:* The mourning dove is among the most common and widespread backyard birds in North America, willing to stay close to consistent food supplies in large flocks.

Primarily a bird of the West, the violet-green swallow catches its insect prey in continuous flights over water or through the treetops. *Below:* In the northern United States and Canada, the tree swallow is the first swallow to return in the spring from its southern migration.

The rufous hummingbird winters in
Mexico and, in limited numbers, along the
U.S. Gulf Coast. *Left:* The ruby-
throated hummingbird is the only hummer
that breeds east of the Mississippi River.
The nest is made of plant down woven
together with spider silk. *Opposite:* The
male of the aptly named broad-billed
hummingbird is so bright red as to appear
fluorescent. The bird inhabits foothill
gullies near desert areas.

Hummers, like this Allen's hummingbird, can flow forward at 30 miles per hour, hover, ascend, descend and even fly backwards. They have enormously developed breast muscles to help with these feats. *Below:* Costa's hummingbird inhabits arid foothills and low desert slopes, where it feeds largely on the nectar of cacti, mesquite, sages and yucca. *Opposite:* Man's domestic flowers and water supplies have enabled substantial growth in the population of Anna's hummingbird, the earliest nesting bird in California.

Because of their smaller size, they also prefer to avoid the rough-housing crowds of mourning doves and starlings that often gather at the other feeders.

And so, I've given them their own feeder. It's visited by other species with a yen for safflower, including evening grosbeaks, titmice and chickadees. But, in my mind, it's there for the cardinals. Their frequent visits to it hint that perhaps they agree.

Such is the addiction that backyard birding can hold. A certain species can grab hold of your soul, for any number of perfectly illogical reasons, and you're trapped. Or every species can touch you in its own way.

Blue jays, hated by some backyard birders, have found their place with me. A few pounds of peanuts in the shell are part of every week's grocery order, just to encourage the antics of these big, raucous, blue birds. What other species makes such an entrance as to scatter the entire feeding assemblage for a moment?

Top to bottom: **Chickadee. In winter, flocks of chickadees establish regular "rounds" of feeders in their territories and often appear to be moving about on a rigid schedule. The brilliant color of the male vermilion flycatcher led Spanish explorers to call it the "little coal of fire." The western wood pewee ranges from Alaska to Mexico and spends the winter months in Mexico south through Bolivia.**

Given the right attitude, one can even smile at the relish with which starlings, house finches, house sparrows, mourning doves and their ilk attack the cheap seed scattered at the base of another feeder.

My home-office window overlooks this wonderland of activity. As a result I get far less written than I probably should.

Even cross-continent travel won't allow the addict to escape this passion for birding. Standing practically among a herd of elk on the lawn at Mammoth Hot Springs Hotel in northern Yellowstone National Park last fall, I found my attention occasionally being drawn away from the eyepiece of my camera to a black-and-white movement in a cluster of trees at my right. Plenty of top-quality shots of elk were already on my film, and I soon found myself adding to them the images of several black-billed magpies. The elk herd was left to the other tourists as I followed this new contrastingly colored quarry.

The eastern phoebe was among the first birds ever banded for study, in 1840 by Audubon. *Right:* Living up to its name, the eastern kingbird is extremely protective of its territory, aggressively challenging and vanquishing much larger birds, even hawks. *Overleaf:* The pileated woodpecker was mainly a bird of the forest, but now lives even on the edges of cities.

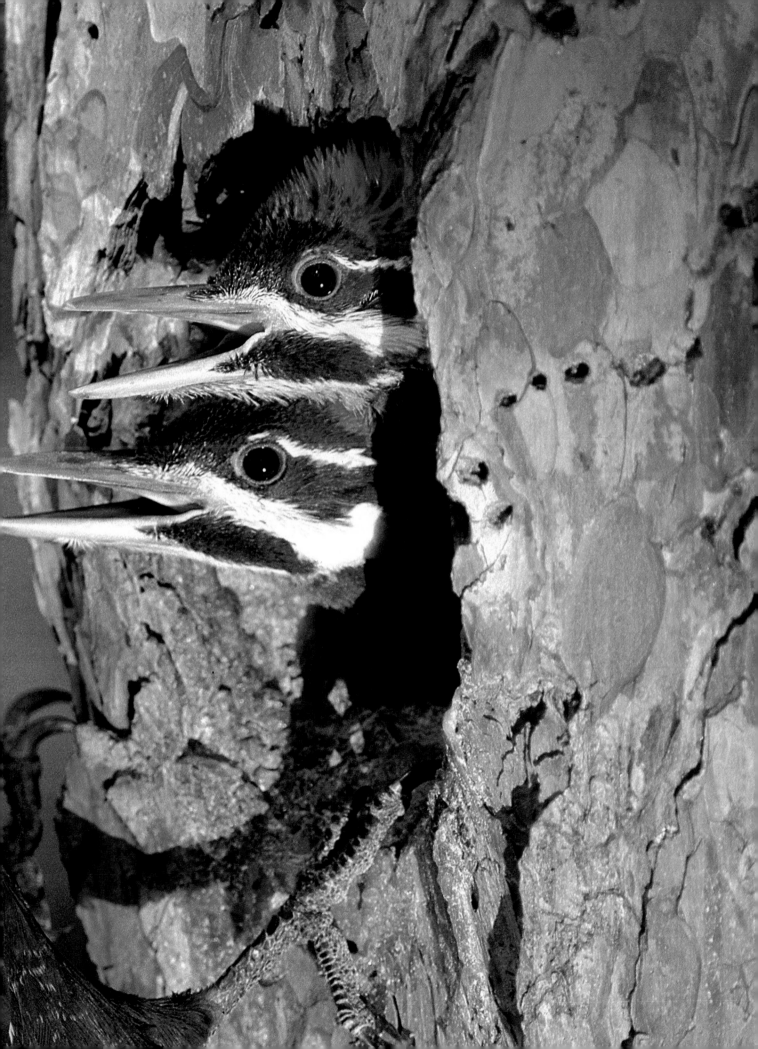

The hairy woodpecker is an extremely beneficial bird, destroying countless insects that are harmful to fruit and lumber trees. *Left:* The golden-fronted woodpecker is resident only of the southwestern United States and is quite common in parks there. *Opposite:* The yellow-bellied sapsucker bores holes into the inner bark of trees to start sap oozing out and down the trunk so it can suck the sap up with its brushlike tongue.

A fascination for the quite common gray jays also developed on this trip. True to their lore, the birds spend every spare minute grabbing food from the picnic tables of unsuspecting tourists, exhibiting a passion for the sport equal to that of cartoonland's Yogi Bear.

But the greatest wonderment still comes in the backyard, where the interaction between the birds themselves, and between the birds and my many manmade contrivances, can at once have an incredible sameness and an immeasurable diversity to it.

A flock of house finches descends on the hanging feeder, occupying every perch available and forcing one another to trade off feeding opportunities. They remain for quite a while, but the quite similar American goldfinch flock engulfs the nearby thistle feeder, gorges for a few minutes and then is gone for several hours.

The red-bellied woodpecker prefers the southeastern U.S. as its habitat. *Right:* **The red-headed woodpecker shares the same region as the red-bellied variety, but is also found as far north as Canada.** *Opposite:* **The common flicker feeding hungry fledglings.**

The chickadees fill the young sugar maple tree, taking turns at plucking a seed or two from the feeder and gliding back to the tree to eat them. A short while later they will be gone, moved to their next "patch" and its concentration of food, a few backyards away.

Blue jays arrive toward mid-morning, streaming straight-away into a platform feeder where peanuts have been served. A few shells will be split and their contents eaten on the spot, but most will be stashed away in the leafy mulch along the hedge-row of barberry.

The cactus wren constructs several false nests on the cacti of its territory, it roosts there under the protection of the spines. *Below:* House wrens often choose manmade cavities, including flower pots, mailboxes, laundry on clotheslines and discarded tin cans, for their next locations.

The mockingbird, the lone male that has claimed this backyard as his territory, dive-bombs all of these interlopers on a daily schedule. His direct attacks are momentarily successful at best, far inferior to the rage he successfully solicits from a robin with his accurate imitation of the robin's song.

Mourning doves, seemingly more of them every day, waddle about the low platform feeder, filling their crops with the cracked corn. Most disturbances, short of a direct attack by a cat or dog, will pass without much notice on their part. Only others of their

The red-breasted nuthatch spreads pine pitch around the entrance to its cavity nest. Why we don't know, but it may involve a protection from predators. *Below:* White-breasted nuthatches are often referred to as the "upside-down" bird because of their feeding habit of descending tree trunks head first.

own kind seem able to draw a response, generally a brief pecking when feeding space has been violated.

So much life going on in such a little space, that's the lure of backyard birding. Estimates of the number of people involved range to 100 million, spending in the billions of dollars on bird seed and assorted paraphernalia.

Northern mockingbirds develop wide-ranging repertoires of songs, mimicking the sounds of other birds as well as non-bird sounds like the human whistle. After these northern mockingbird nestlings have been fledged, the dominant parent bird often will drive them, and its mate, from its territory.

Sport, pastime, passion, whatever description is appropriate, backyard birding is among the easiest to begin. Toss a few handfuls of grocery-store bird seed onto the ground each morning or into a plastic bin-type feeder on a pole and you're involved. Some of the local birds will take an interest in your offerings.

But few people stay at that first level. More elaborate feeders, each designed for its own purpose, beckon. Opportunities to attract certain colorful species cry out. And soon the newcomer is among the one in three American families that put out an average of 60 pounds of bird seed every year.

The true impact of all this easy and abundant food on the birds is a highly debated topic. Some species, such as the northern cardinal and the house finch, appear to have expanded the northern extents of their ranges in a correlation to the increase in feeding over the past three decades. And without a doubt, some weaker

Top to bottom: **The hermit thrush switches its basic diet from insects in the warmer months to berries and buds during the winter. The varied thrush. The western meadowlark, its song is often part of background effects on movie soundtracks.**

or sickly individual birds do make it through the tough winter months because of the helping human hand. But some experts feel that bird feeding satisfies more human needs than bird needs.

But no one can debate the fact that feeding will bring more birds to a backyard and keep them there longer, or that certain types of bird seed accomplish this task better than others.

The definitive statement of what seed works best was answered in a study conducted by Aelred D. Geis of the U.S. Fish & Wildlife Service. Cited so often that it is now simply called the Geis Study, the work involved volunteer bird feeders/observers in California, Maine, Maryland and Ohio, as well as hundreds of thousands of feeders. The conclusion: The best bird seed depends on the birds you want to attract.

Top to bottom: Orange segments are a popular backyard feeder food for the northern oriole, which until recently was known as the Baltimore oriole. Most nests of the hooded oriole will contain at least one egg of the bronzed cowbird, which regularly deposits its eggs in the oriole's nest and leaves the rearing chores to the other bird. Famous symbol of spring, some American robins are actually present year-round in much of the United States. In the northern part of the country, however, they do spend much of the winter in heavily forested areas. The northern oriole constructs a hanging sack of a nest from plant fibers, string, bits of plastic bags and twigs.

Oil-type sunflower seeds were the first choice of chickadees, evening grosbeaks, mourning doves, northern cardinals and purple finches. Peanut kernels were preferred by blue jays, tufted titmice and white-throated sparrows.

Hulled sunflower seeds were number one with American goldfinches and white-crowned sparrows. Black-stripe sunflower seeds were favored by common grackles. White proso millet attracted brown-headed cowbirds, house finches and mourning doves. And, red proso millet was preferred only by mourning doves.

A male red-winged blackbird mounts a territorial display, warning other males that they are intruding on his turf. Although primarily a marshland species, its nests can be found near almost any body of water. *Opposite:* Yellow-headed blackbirds nest in crowded colonies, where predators are mobbed and driven off.

European starlings.

Maybe even more importantly, the Geis Study discovered that hulled oats, peanut hearts, rice and wheat — common ingredients in many cheap, bulk-package, grocery store, wild bird mixes — had virtually no appeal for any species.

Just as a blend of the proper seeds is needed to attract a variety of species into the backyard, a diverse collection of feeders will serve the many different preferences in feeding arrangements.

The totally equipped backyard will feature a hanging or pole feeder filled with oil-type sunflower seeds, a hanging thistle seed feeder, a ground feeder or low tray feeder with cracked corn and mixed seeds, and a suet feeder. A source of water, such as a bird bath or a small garden pond, will enhance the attracting ability of any feeder arrangement.

Top to bottom: **The Brewer's blackbird spends much of the winter near farms, where it eats any grain or animal feed that is spilled. Common grackles have an incredibly diverse diet, ranging from grains to small animals like mice and frogs to garbage scavenged from litter baskets. The clearing of much of North America's forests has been a boon to the common crow, whose population has skyrocketed.**

This page: The Steller's jay spends much of its time eating seeds and insects high in the top limbs of pine trees. It carries the habit of long-jumping from branch to branch with it to ground level when it descends to scavenge picnic scraps.
Right: The gray jay will also scavenge unattended campgrounds. *Opposite:* Blue jays often stow seeds in the crooks of trees for later use.

The loggerhead shrike, also known as the butcher bird, impales its prey, such as rodents and small birds, on thorns or barbed wire. *Left:* The cedar waxwing travels in flocks for most of the year, moving from area to area, finding and exhausting the local berry crops.

Evening grosbeaks can be bullies at the feeder, but many backyard birders accept that behavior in exchange for their bright colors. *Right:* The rose-breasted grosbeak makes a metallic clinking call that is easily recognized.

The western tanager spends much of
its time feeding in the tops of tall
conifers. *Right:* The red crossbill can
easily pluck seeds from conifer cones,
their exclusive food source, with its
unusual bill. *Opposite:* Pine grosbeaks
allow close approach and then escape
slowly to a short distance away.

Lazuli bunting. *Below:* Painted buntings were popular cage birds in the last century, before they came under federal protection. *Opposite:* Courting pairs of northern cardinals frequently pass seeds and other small bits of food to one another, beak to beak.

Responding to an ever-hungry market, the multi-billion-dollar birding industry has also developed many specialized feeders. A window feeder, much like an aquarium placed on its side and inserted into a window in the home, will bring some of the tamer birds – chickadees, nuthatches and titmice – practically into the room for close-up viewing. Bottles with tiny outlets and perches, to be filled with sugar-water solutions, will attract and feed the energetic hummingbirds. Fruit-holding feeders are designed for specialized preferences, like those of the oriole.

It's increasingly easy to spend several hundred dollars over the course of a year to attract birds, but the rewards reaped for each additional aspect built into the backyard habitat can't be measured in dollars and cents. Unfolding every day is the real "real world," the struggle for survival in all its dimensions.

The eastern bluebird was in severe decline earlier in this century, until efforts were made to provide it with manmade nesting cavities. *Left:* Where European starlings and house sparrows are brought under control, eastern bluebirds will nest as thickly as a pair to an acre.

The cardinal-like pyrrhuloxia is a resident of mesquite thickets, where it feeds primarily on mesquite beans. *Below:* A trio of mountain bluebirds, western counterparts of the eastern bluebird, enjoy a splash in a mountain brook.

"Attack" is an appropriate description when a flock of common redpolls enters a patch of winter-dry weeds, tearing the stalks to pieces and retrieving the released seeds from the ground. *Below:* The dark-eyed junco is among the most common of backyard feeder visitors.

The bright lemon-yellow plumage of the male American goldfinch fades to a dull olive-drab for the late fall and winter. *Below:* Watch the leaf litter under hedgerows for the rufous-sided towhee.

Large flocks of purple finches consistently visit feeders throughout the winter, taking oil-type sunflower seeds with relish.

Sometimes the struggle can be as dramatic as the lightning-fast attack from out of the sky by a sharp-shinned hawk and the resulting death of a chickadee. Or the body-less wail of a screech owl winging its way through the black night sky in search of its next rodent meal.

At other times it's as comical as the shifting and edging of a flock of European starlings as they settle onto a power line, each one insisting on a social space of four or five inches between itself and those on either side of it.

Within that wide range is a whole world of activity to be observed, questioned and understood. Each species brings its own special life style with it into the backyard, adding to the richness that already exists and expanding on it by its presence.

Top to bottom: **The song sparrow can be found nearly everywhere on the North American continent. The house finch is a native species of the West. It became established in the East from a few captive birds that escaped in New York City in the 1940s. Experiments in the laboratory with the white-crowned sparrow have revealed much of our current knowledge of the physical aspects of migration.**

When threatened, the savannah sparrow prefers to drop into the tall grasses. *Below:* A chipping sparrow parent offers a caterpillar meal to its nearly grown offspring. *Opposite:* Screaming, hungry, yellow warbler babies keep a parent bird busy throughout the weeks until they go off on their own.

Song sparrows of the neighborhood share communal bits of their song patterns. Each bird has its own repertoire of a dozen or more songs, but certain elements will be common to all the birds of the local community. Some nestlings may even try to get in on the game before they've learned to fly. The lucky listener can actually hear them passing the notes along to one another.

The blue jay drops onto an anthill and waits for the attacking insects to crawl among its feathers, even picking some of the ants up in its beak and inserting them into itself. The bird then throws itself into a violent episode of preening under its wings and along its tails. Various theories for this "anting" behavior include use of the formic acid from the ants to ward off parasites, sensual pleasure and a treatment for irritated skin.

Top to bottom: **A principal victim of the cowbird, which deposits its eggs in the nests of other birds, the yellow warbler often responds by building a new nest bottom right over the interloping egg and sometimes its own eggs. The Wilson's warbler stays quite close to ground level, pursuing its insect prey on the wing. The Myrtle's warbler is the only warbler that winters in the northeastern United States.** *Opposite:* **The first specimen of the Cape May warbler was discovered at the New Jersey beach resort community, hence its name.**

The common yellowthroat. *Below:* Second-stage thicket growth taking over abandoned pastures has helped spread the chestnut-sided warbler population.

Half of the pair of house wrens that have set up housekeeping in the mailbox – necessitating the construction of a second box for the delivery of the mail – darts from that postal home to the flower bed. Seconds later, with a freshly caught insect in its beak, it returns to its screaming, hungry brood.

American robins on the hunt for earthworms bounce through the grass, cocking their heads at each stop and then grabbing their prey or bouncing a bit farther. Popular lore holds that the birds are listening for the worms. But they are actually cocking their heads to get a better view because their eyes are planted squarely on the sides of their heads.

Leaf litter flies from beneath the barberry hedge as a brown thrasher thrashes about with its beak, in search of its own insect meal.

A white-breasted nuthatch again earns its reputation as ”the upside-down bird” by clambering down a tree trunk head- first. It pecks at the cracks in the bark as it moves, plucking away hapless insects.

The chickadees become so tame as to take seed from a human hand. They're always among the last to flee the feeder in the face of a threat, allowing close approach by their human benefactor. A few

The red-eyed vireo is among the most abundant species in the East.

This page and opposite: A flock of mallards explodes from the surface of a pond. Two mallard drakes dip to pluck succulent plants from the bottom of the pond. Mallard ducks are extremely strong fliers, occasionally reaching oceanic islands and establishing new populations.

seeds tossed their way on a few occasions followed by an open hand filled with seed is often all it takes to spur the direct bird-human contact.

A ruby-throated hummingbird darts onto the scene, at first passing the red plastic hummer feeder. He stops in mid- air, hovers for a moment and then backs up to the source of sugar-rich water.

The male American goldfinch loses his brilliant, lemon-yellow plumage of the warmer months for dull olive-drab feathers in late fall and winter. His change back to the bright "salad bird" of summer will be among the first signals that winter is losing its grip on the land.

Two common grackles settle their differences through a showy display of their physiques, pushing out their chests, puffing their feathers and tossing their head back to point directly skyward with their bills. No blows are exchanged, but within seconds the dispute is past and both birds are feeding peacefully once again.

The four-inch, male painted bunting dives repeatedly at the couple of crows that have landed to grab a few scattered bread crumbs.

Eventually the larger birds give way to their tiny nemesis, allowing him this territory he has claimed for the nesting season. Had the territorial insult come from another male bunting, a fight to the death might have ensued. As it is, the crows were merely inconvenienced.

In another season, with a late afternoon snowstorm approaching, the entire back-yard complement turns out. Feeding will take on a frenzied atmosphere. Each member of the community hurries to build up what limited reserves its small body can muster for the cold and stormy night ahead.

A flock of ring-necked pheasants sneaks through the hedgerow to the cracked corn scattered on the ground. The male, distinguished from the sandy brown females by his iridescent purple and green head and his shimmering body feathers, is the source of that distant cackling each morning.

Top to bottom: **The ruddy duck prefers to dive out of sight or to hide among vegetation rather than flight to escape threats. Unlike most waterfowl, wood ducks nest in tree cavities rather than among ground vegetation. The pintail is among our most cautious ducks because of its popularity as a gamebird.** *Opposite:* **Nearly every pothole on the prairies of the Midwest will host a nesting pair of blue-winged teal (top). The Canada goose population is booming as the huge bird takes advantage of the protected ponds in man's parks and the profusion of easy food offered by well-meaning people (bottom).**

If the backyard is near a pond or slow-moving river, a flock of Canada geese or mallard ducks might waddle by. Once mostly migratory, large numbers of these birds have taken up permanent residence in parks throughout the East. Held there largely by man's usually abundant offerings of bread crumbs, crackers and other goodies, the birds often become a problem for nearby residents.

The range of activity continues on, well beyond these few common species and the capacity of any one book to catalog and describe. That, too, is part of the charm of the backyard birding world.

The American kestrel, the most adapted to man of all the North American hawks, makes its home in towns and cities and preys largely on the house sparrow. *Left:* Cooper's hawks were among the raptors that suffered severe population declines because of man's proliferation of pesticides. *Opposite:* American kestrels, or sparrow hawks, are small and seemingly delicate for a bird of prey.

A red-tailed hawk tends its nest of down-covered young. In the wake of the declining Cooper's hawk, the sharp-shinned hawk is now the most common species in North America. *Opposite:* Red-tailed hawks often perch on the upper limbs of tall trees at the edge of meadows, which they survey for rodent prey.

Gambel's quail adjust their breeding and nesting season to coincide with the growth of vegetation in the semiarid regions they inhabit. Dry years may result in no nesting at all. *Below:* The ring-necked pheasant is in decline across much of the continent because of modern farming practices that eliminate fencerows and other areas of cover. *Opposite:* The northern bobwhite, which extends about as far north as southern Pennsylvania, is easily identified by its namesake call.

Index of Photography